W9-AVH-046

WITHDRAWN

FUN FACT FILE:
ANIMALS!

# 20 FUN FACTS ABOUT

# SHARKS

By Heather Moore Niver

Gareth Stevens
Publishing

Please visit our website, www.garethstevens.com. For a free color catalog of all our high-quality books, call toll free 1-800-542-2595 or fax 1-877-542-2596.

Library of Congress Cataloging-in-Publication Data

Niver, Heather Moore.
20 fun facts about sharks / Heather Moore Niver.
    p. cm. — (Fun fact file. Animals!)
Includes index.
ISBN 978-1-4339-6527-2 (pbk.)
ISBN 978-1-4339-6528-9 (6-pack)
ISBN 978-1-4339-6525-8 (library binding)
1.  Sharks—Miscellanea—Juvenile literature.  I. Title. II. Title: Twenty fun facts about sharks.
QL638.9.N58 2012
597.3—dc23

                                    2011036638


First Edition

Published in 2012 by
**Gareth Stevens Publishing**
111 East 14th Street, Suite 349
New York, NY 10003

Copyright © 2012 Gareth Stevens Publishing

Designer: Michael J. Flynn
Editor: Greg Roza

Photo credits: Cover, pp. 1, 5, 6, 9, 10, 12, 13, 14, 15, 17, 18, 20–21, 23, 24, 25, 26, 27, 29 Shutterstock.com; pp. 7, 22 iStockphoto.com; p. 8 Ian Waldie/Getty Images; p. 11 Richard Herrmann/Visuals Unlimited/Getty Images; p. 16 Jeff Rotoman/Iconica/ Getty Images; p. 19 Andy Murch/Visuals Unlimited/Getty Images.

All rights reserved. No part of this book may be reproduced in any form without permission in writing from the publisher, except by a reviewer.

Printed in the United States of America

CPSIA compliance information: Batch #CW12GS: For further information contact Gareth Stevens, New York, New York at 1-800-542-2595.

# Contents

Words in the glossary appear in **bold** type the first time they are used in the text.

# Fish to Fear

Sharks are scary creatures. They're sharp-toothed hunters. When beachgoers see a triangle-shaped fin sticking out of the water, they get nervous. On television and in movies, swimmers usually race screaming out of the water.

Yes, sharks can be dangerous animals. Swimmers are wise to stay a safe distance from these big, toothy fish. But not all sharks are to be feared. In fact, three of the largest sharks mainly eat tiny sea creatures called plankton!

You can probably tell by its name that the whale shark is the largest of all sharks. And pygmy sharks are some of the smallest.

whale shark

## FACT 1

## Sharks were swimming in the oceans before dinosaurs walked Earth.

The first sharks lived over 300 million years ago! Modern sharks are probably related to sharks from 100 million to 70 million years ago, and they haven't changed much since ancient times. The ancient shark called megalodon was more than 45 feet (13.7 m) long!

This is a megalodon tooth. Now imagine a whole mouth full of these giant teeth!

# Chomp!

## Sharks are almost always losing teeth.

Shark teeth are replaced with new ones every 8 days. A shark can lose as many as 30,000 teeth during its life! Different sharks have different kinds of teeth. Whale sharks have very short teeth because they don't eat fish. Some sharks have teeth for crushing shells.

Despite having so many sharp teeth, sharks don't use their teeth for chewing. They use them for catching and tearing food.

7

When a shark dies, the salty ocean water breaks down its body until only its teeth are left!

# FACT 3

## Sharks don't have any bones.

A shark's **skeleton** isn't made of bone. It's made of **cartilage**. You have cartilage in your body, too. Your nose and ears are mostly cartilage. Cartilage bends more easily than bone. Scientists study shark cartilage because it may be useful in medicine.

# Sink or Swim

**Great white, mako, and salmon sharks drown if they don't keep swimming.**

Unlike other fish, sharks don't have a **swim bladder**. If they didn't keep swimming, they'd sink to the ocean floor. Great white, mako, and salmon sharks need to swim all the time to keep water passing over their **gill** slits. If they didn't keep swimming, they'd drown!

Sharks have five to seven gill slits on each side of their heads.

9

# Although most sharks swim in warm ocean water, some can be found in cold water or freshwater.

Hundreds of species, or kinds, of sharks live in oceans all over the world. Most live in warm or tropical waters, but a few swim in colder water. Greenland sharks swim in icy Arctic waters. Bull sharks do very well in freshwater.

Scientists keep discovering new shark species. Some believe there might be more than 500 kinds of sharks!

**bull shark**

Sharks can swim hundreds of miles in a single day.

**mako shark**

## FACT 6

## The mako is the fastest shark.

Sharks are at home in the water, and these fish can swim fast! Almost all sharks can swim between 20 and 30 miles (32 and 48 km) per hour. The mako whooshes through the water at 60 miles (97 km) per hour!

A hammerhead school can have hundreds of sharks. Most of them are female.

## FACT 7

# Sharks are most active after the sun goes down.

Some sharks, such as hammerheads, swim in groups known as schools. But most sharks like to swim and hunt on their own. Scientists have found that sharks are most active just after the sun goes down and at night.

# Shark Shape

Some scientists think hammerhead sharks' strange head helps them swim. Other scientists think it helps them find and catch fish.

## FACT 8

### A shark's shape helps it swim faster.

Most sharks have the same basic shape. It's called fusiform. They have narrow **snouts** and tails, and their bodies are wider in the middle. This shape helps them speed through the water without using too much energy.

A shark's dorsal fins allow it to keep its balance in the water. Dorsal fins also help a shark to turn.

## FACT 9

# Sharks have something in common with airplanes.

A shark's powerful tail fin keeps it moving forward, similar to a plane's **propeller**. Water rushing over a shark's pectoral fins creates a force called lift, which keeps it from sinking. This is the same force created when air rushes over an airplane's wings!

# SHARK PARTS

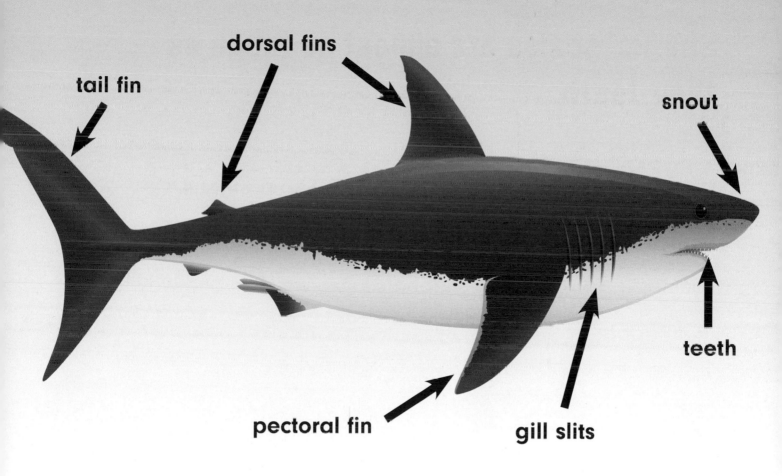

tail fin

dorsal fins

snout

pectoral fin

gill slits

teeth

# Lookin' Sharp!

## FACT 10

### Sharks' scales are almost as tough as their teeth.

Sharks have strong skin that protects them. It's covered by sharp, tooth-like scales called denticles. The denticles can almost overlap, or they can be spaced farther apart. Different species have differently shaped scales, which is one way to tell them apart.

Shark skin is so rough it's used as sandpaper.

The leopard shark has black spots and long, flowing fins.

**FACT 11**

## Sharks are colorful creatures.

Sharks are all kinds of colors. They can be blue, red-brown, black, or gray. Lots of sharks have stripes or spots. Others are marbled, which means they have swirls and spots of color like the stone with that name.

This blacktip reef shark swims near the water's surface while hunting for a meal.

# FACT 12

## Shark colors help them hide when hunting.

Most sharks have light-colored bellies. They look like the sky to **prey** swimming below them. Darker skin on their backs makes them harder to see from above, because they blend in with the dark water. This is called countershading.

# Time for Dinner!

## FACT 13

## A shark's diet is never boring.

Sharks eat lots of things, so dinner is almost never dull. Of course, different sharks eat different things. They eat plankton, clams, crabs, and even sea turtles. Sharks also chow down on fish, seals, porpoises, and whales, too!

**basking shark**

Whale sharks and basking sharks eat by straining plankton through their gills.

The tiger shark is one of the most dangerous sharks.

## FACT 14

# Each year, more people are killed by bees than by sharks.

Sharks are dangerous **predators**, but the chance of being killed by one is pretty low. Only 20 species of sharks are known to attack humans. They usually only hurt people, not kill them. In fact, more people are killed by bees each year than by sharks!

## FACT 15

## Some sharks can push their stomach out of their mouth.

A shark stomach can hold a lot of food. Some sharks can

push their belly out of their mouth! They do this to empty their

stomach after eating something that makes them sick.

Balloon sharks fill their belly with air or water when

they're scared.

# Baby, Baby!

## Some sharks have hundreds of babies at a time.

Shark babies are called pups. Not all pups are born the same way. Some hatch from eggs. Others grow inside the mother. Mother sharks usually have between two and 20 pups at a time. Whale sharks can have up to 300 pups!

Shark eggs don't look like bird eggs. However, you can see the yolk and baby shark growing inside this shark egg.

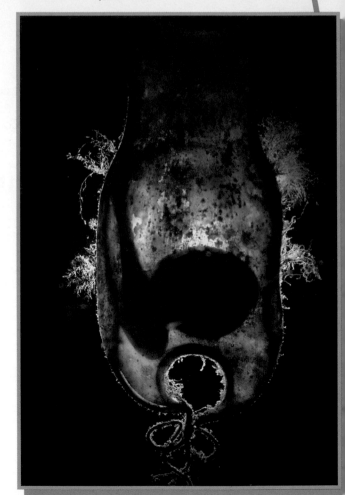

# Shark Senses

**A great white shark can smell one drop of blood in an Olympic-size swimming pool.**

Of its five senses, the shark's sense of smell is the best. The shark uses around 70 percent of its brain for its sense of smell. Sharks can use smell to find their prey. The hungrier they are, the better they can smell!

Sharks have eyes on the sides of their head, so they can see almost all the way around them.

# FACT 18

## Some sharks have special eyes to help them see better.

Sharks have very good eyesight. They can see well even when water is dark or cloudy. Some sharks have a special layer inside their eyes that acts like a mirror. This shines more light into the eye and helps them see better.

# A shark knows that a "yummy hum" means a quick meal is nearby.

Injured fish make a sound too low for people to hear.

However, sharks can hear this "yummy hum." Sharks can also

feel changes in water pressure when something swims by,

almost as if it has touched them.

Hungry sharks sometimes fight over prey.

A shark's electricity-sensing organs are located in its head and snout.

# FACT 20

## Sharks can sense electricity.

As if they weren't already deadly enough, sharks can sense electricity produced by passing prey. This helps them locate a meal even in dark or cloudy water. Sharks can also sense Earth's **magnetic field**, which may help them steer when moving.

# SHARKS BY THE NUMBERS

| | | |
|---|---|---|
| Some sharks live to be 100 years old. | There are 350 known species of sharks. | The megamouth shark has only been spotted 41 times. The first time was in 1976. |
| Sharks can replace lost teeth in as little as 24 hours. | A great white shark eats 11 tons of food each year. | Sharks can hear their prey from more than 800 feet (244 m) away. |
| Shark fin soup, popular in China, results in the deaths of more than 73 million sharks each year. | The pygmy shark only grows to about 8 inches (20 cm) long. | The frilled shark has more than 300 teeth. |

# Beyond the Bite

It may seem like there are plenty of sharks in the ocean. However, around 20 percent of sharks are **endangered**, mainly because of too much fishing. Many are killed by mistake when they're caught in fishing nets and on hooks.

Once you get past the teeth, sharks are pretty interesting animals. Their skills have kept them swimming in our oceans for millions of years. Safer fishing practices are needed to help protect sharks so they can stay around even longer.

Bull sharks live in warm, coastal waters. They're one of the sharks most likely to attack people.

# Glossary

**cartilage:** a stretchy tissue that makes up part or all of a skeleton

**endangered:** in danger of dying out

**gill:** an organ that sharks and other fish use to get oxygen from the water

**magnetic field:** the area around a magnet where its pull is felt. Earth has a magnetic field, too.

**predator:** an animal that hunts other animals for food

**prey:** an animal that is hunted by other animals for food

**propeller:** paddle-like parts on a plane that spin to move the plane forward

**skeleton:** the strong frame that supports an animal's body

**snout:** a long nose that sticks out

**swim bladder:** a sac in a fish that holds air and keeps the fish from sinking

# For More Information

## Books

Llewellyn, Claire. *The Best Book of Sharks.* Boston, MA: Kingfisher, 2005.

MacQuitty, Miranda. *Shark.* New York, NY: DK Publishing, 2008.

Smith, Miranda. *Sharks.* New York, NY: Kingfisher, 2008.

## Websites

### Great White Sharks
*kids.nationalgeographic.com/kids/animals/creaturefeature/great-white-shark/*
Learn more about great white sharks and other animals, too, with facts, maps, videos, and more.

### Shark Week
*dsc.discovery.com/tv/shark-week/*
Check out shark facts, games, videos, puzzles, and lots more on the Discovery Channel's website.

**Publisher's note to educators and parents:** Our editors have carefully reviewed these websites to ensure that they are suitable for students. Many websites change frequently, however, and we cannot guarantee that a site's future contents will continue to meet our high standards of quality and educational value. Be advised that students should be closely supervised whenever they access the Internet.

# Index